RAINY DAY BOOK

Books from OWL are published in Canada by
Greey de Pencier Books, 56 The Esplanade,
Suite 306, Toronto, Ontario M5E 1A7.

Published simultaneously in the United States by
Firefly Books (U.S.) Inc.
P.O. Box 1338, Ellicott Station, Buffalo, NY 14205

Originally published in Australia by Ellsyd Press.

*trademarks of the Young Naturalist Foundation.

Canadian Cataloguing in Publication Data

Ingram, Anne Bower
Rainy day book

Canadian ed.
Originally published in Australia under title:
Family car fun book.
ISBN 0-920775-44-6

1. Amusements – Juvenile literature.
2. Indoor games – Juvenile literature.
3. Creative activities and seat work – Juvenile literature.
I. O'Donnell, Peggy. II. Peters, Shirley.
III. Title. IV. Title: Rainy day fun book.

GV1203.I54 1990   j793'01.'922   C89-090650-5

Cover design by Wycliffe Smith
Cover photo by Ray Boudreau
Cover illustration by Vesna Krstanovich

Printed in Hong Kong
B C D E F G

RAINY DAY BOOK

Anne Ingram
&
Peggy O'Donnell

Illustrations by
Shirley Peters

OWL

Greey de Pencier Books

Our Granddaughters
Melissa and Stephanie

Contents

It's Raining!

It's raining again! But that's great, now you can try all these fabulous ideas we've gathered together for you.

While it's raining at home, there are places in the world where people are trying to make it rain. Nowadays scientists have developed chemicals, which they release into particular cloud formations, to try and make it rain. This is called "seeding the clouds".

Throughout history there are records of "rainmakers", people who claim they can make it rain by singing a few secret incantations, performing a special rain dance, or by using a variety of magic potions. Their rate of success is not recorded in any great detail.

Even today, with all our technology, we still cannot make it rain where it's needed, or turn it off when we've had enough.

Rainy day trivia

The tradition of giving hurricanes and cyclones female names started in the United States during World War II. One story has it that during a storm warning an American radio operator was whistling *Every little breeze seems to whisper Louise.* Immediately the storm was christened "Louise", and the custom continued up to the 70s when the World Meteorological Society decided to use alternate male and female names.

The human brain is 80 per cent water.

Almost one-eighth of the earth's surface receives less than 25 cm (9¾ in) of rain a year.

Rubber boots were first worn during the Napoleonic Wars by the Duke of Wellington. They were named after him when they came into general use.

In England, during the early part of this century, farmers were able to buy Wellington boots (wellies) for their sheep. They thought they would stop foot diseases!

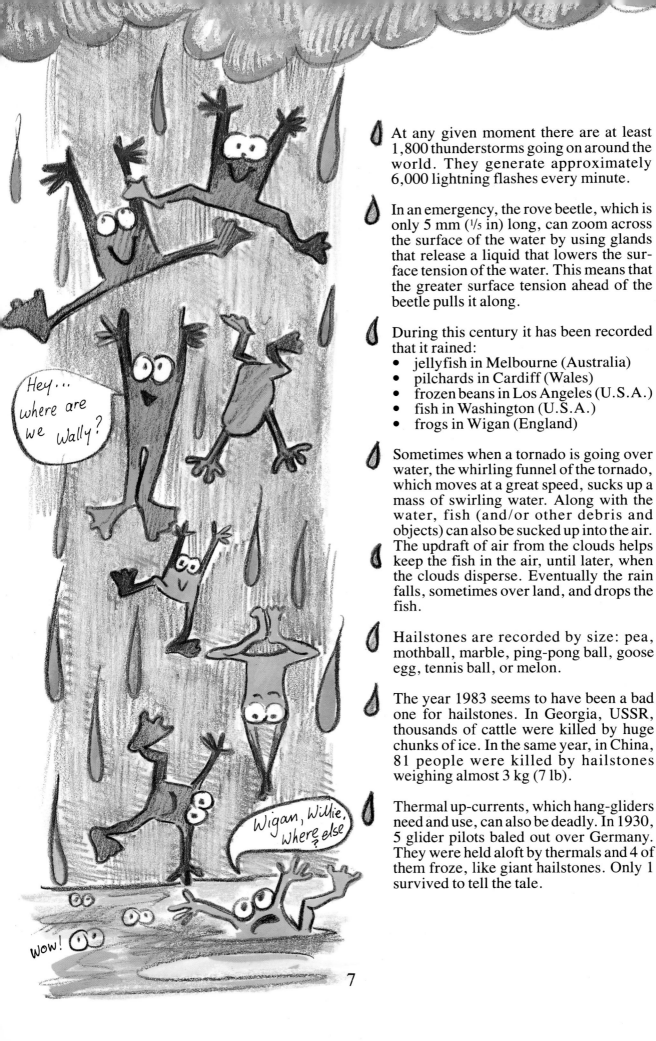

At any given moment there are at least 1,800 thunderstorms going on around the world. They generate approximately 6,000 lightning flashes every minute.

In an emergency, the rove beetle, which is only 5 mm (1/5 in) long, can zoom across the surface of the water by using glands that release a liquid that lowers the surface tension of the water. This means that the greater surface tension ahead of the beetle pulls it along.

During this century it has been recorded that it rained:
- jellyfish in Melbourne (Australia)
- pilchards in Cardiff (Wales)
- frozen beans in Los Angeles (U.S.A.)
- fish in Washington (U.S.A.)
- frogs in Wigan (England)

Sometimes when a tornado is going over water, the whirling funnel of the tornado, which moves at a great speed, sucks up a mass of swirling water. Along with the water, fish (and/or other debris and objects) can also be sucked up into the air. The updraft of air from the clouds helps keep the fish in the air, until later, when the clouds disperse. Eventually the rain falls, sometimes over land, and drops the fish.

Hailstones are recorded by size: pea, mothball, marble, ping-pong ball, goose egg, tennis ball, or melon.

The year 1983 seems to have been a bad one for hailstones. In Georgia, USSR, thousands of cattle were killed by huge chunks of ice. In the same year, in China, 81 people were killed by hailstones weighing almost 3 kg (7 lb).

Thermal up-currents, which hang-gliders need and use, can also be deadly. In 1930, 5 glider pilots baled out over Germany. They were held aloft by thermals and 4 of them froze, like giant hailstones. Only 1 survived to tell the tale.

7

Rainy Day Game

Finish	100	99	98	97
80	81	82	83	84
79	78	77	76	75
58	59	60	61	62
57	56	55	54	53
36	37	38	39	40
35	34	33	32	31
17				18
16				15
1				2

How to play:
You need 2 or more players, 1 dice and a counter for each player. Throw the dice and the player with the highest score begins.

Move from start to finish, taking it in turns to throw the dice. If you land at the foot of a rainbow, then follow it to the top. If you land on the top of the lightning, go down to the bottom.

First to arrive at the finish is the winner.

START

SHOWERS

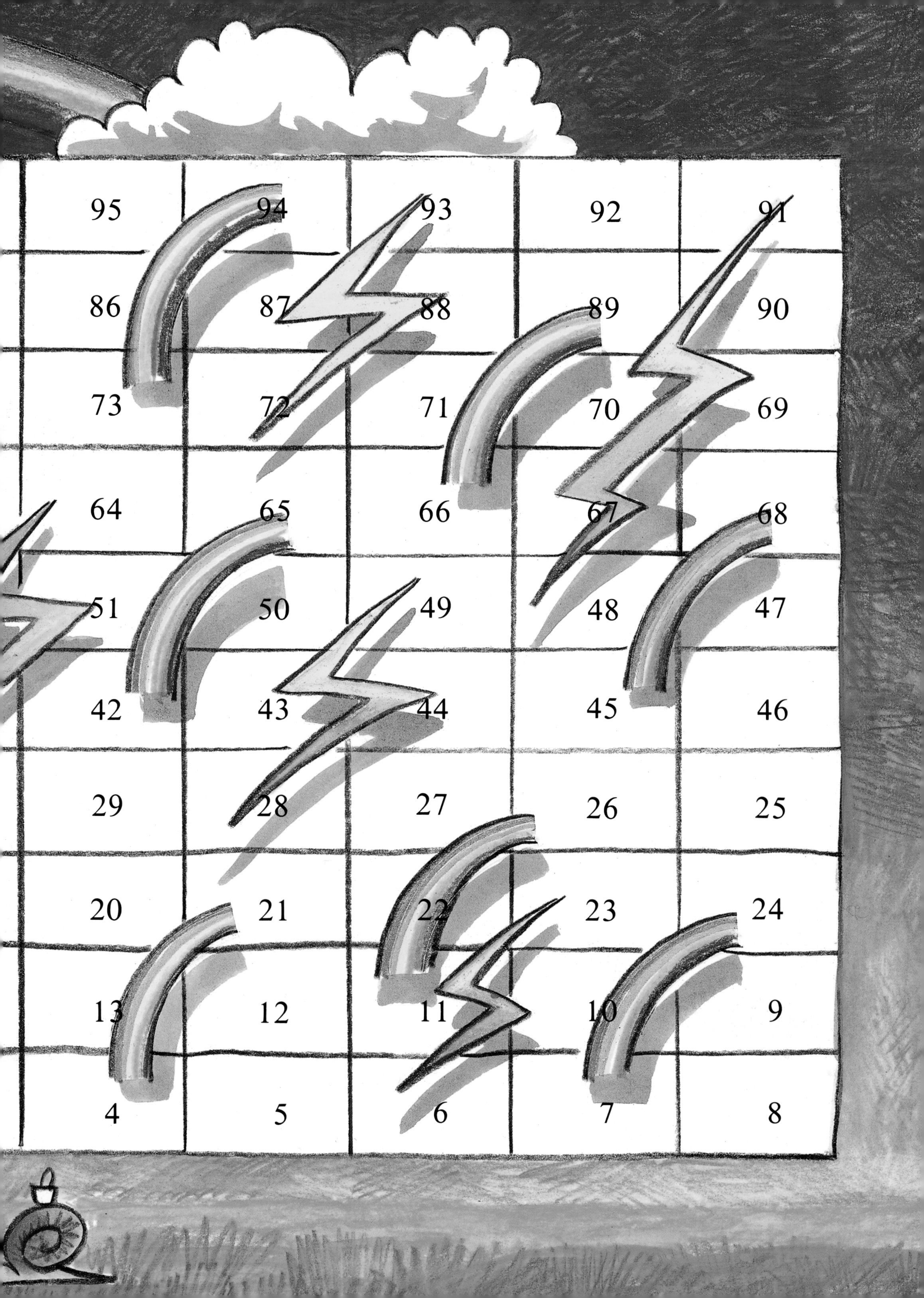
95
94
93
92
91
86
87
88
89
90
73
72
71
70
69
64
65
66
67
68
51
50
49
48
47
42
43
44
45
46
29
28
27
26
25
20
21
22
23
24
13
12
11
10
9
4
5
6
7
8

Before the Rain Begins

The clouds are building up and it certainly looks as if it's about to rain for days. Now is the time to set up a few experiments which you can only do when it's been raining.

Build a rain gauge

You will need:
> tin can, opened at top (without a lip)
> block of wood (or wooden box)
> ruler
> tall glass jar with straight sides
> (an olive jar is ideal)
> felt-tip pen (waterproof)

How to make:
To get a true reading of the rainfall, a rain gauge needs to be set up in an open part of the garden—well away from trees, the house or fences.

The block of wood you use needs to be solid so that the tin can, which is placed in the centre, will sit firmly. The open top of the can needs to be about 30 cm (12 in) above the ground when it's sitting on the wood. Since the can does not have a narrow neck it's more accurate for collecting rainwater.

The next step is to calibrate (mark a scale on) the jar so that you can take accurate measurements of the rainfall.

Fill the can with water to a depth of 10 mm (4 in). Pour this into the jar, making sure you don't spill a drop. Mark the water level on the jar with a felt-tip pen (as shown).

Carefully divide the distance between the water level and the bottom of the jar into 10 equal parts. Each section indicates 1 mm ($\frac{1}{16}$ in) of rain when you pour the contents of the can into the jar.

Continue your measurements up the jar so that when there is a downpour of rain you will be able to take a reading.

When you have collected a day's worth of rain water in the can, pour it into the glass jar to measure the rainfall.

To keep your own daily rainfall chart, draw a chart following this design. It's fun!

10

Cover stops rain

Hole in ground

Uneven rain

This experiment shows how unevenly rain will fall over your garden. Ask if you can borrow 6 or more plastic cups, all the same size. Place these in various positions all around the garden:

- near the wall of the house
- under the drip-line of a tree
- in the middle of the lawn
- under a thick shrub

When the rain has stopped take a measuring jug and check out each container. You will find some of the cups are full, while others are almost empty. This information is handy to have when you're gardening, because you will know exactly where to plant the shrubs that don't need much water.

What comes out in the rain?

The insects and other small creatures that enjoy the wet are very different from the ones you will see in your garden on a dry, sunny day. Now is your chance to capture a few, study them, and then let them go. So, before the rain begins, build this simple trap in the corner of a garden bed.

You will need:

> glass jar without lid
> piece of meat, fish or cheese
> piece of wood
> 4 stones

How to make:
Bury the glass jar, up to its neck, in the corner of the garden. Put the bait in the bottom of the jar. Rest the piece of wood on the 4 stones (as shown), so that it prevents the rain from filling the jar and drowning the insects, but the space at the top between wood and stones allows the insects to crawl in.

When the rain has stopped, check your trap and see what you have caught. During wet weather it will most likely be snails, slugs and other such creatures which thrive in the rain. Place one on a piece of glass, then look at it from below—it moves in a special way.

Remember: As soon as you've made your notes, always let the creature go as near as possible to where you caught it.

Rain and Rainbows

Why does it rain?

Rain is made when the heat of the sun causes the water in the oceans, lakes and rivers to evaporate and rise into the air as water vapour.

As this warm, wet air rises it cools at a high level and forms into clouds. In this cold air the water vapour condenses and becomes drops of water. These stay in the clouds until they are too heavy for them to hold. When this happens — it rains.

Make your own rain

You will need:
  kettle
  water
  ice blocks
  saucepan

Ask an adult to help!

How to make:
Fill the kettle with water and bring it to the boil. Put the ice blocks in the saucepan. When the kettle is boiling and the steam is coming out of the spout at a good speed, carefully hold the saucepan above the spout, keeping your hand well away from the steam.

Watch the bottom of the saucepan. Here you will see drops of water begin to form. They will grow larger and, when they are heavy enough, they will fall and you will be making your own rain.

Make your own rainbow

You will need:
  scissors
  tray or large plastic lid
  white cardboard or
     heavy drawing paper
  red, yellow and blue paint
  paint brush
  7 small jars or lids

How to make:
All the materials you use to make your own rainbow must be suitable to leave out in the rain for a few minutes.

Cut the cardboard or heavy drawing paper, so that it will fit easily into the tray or plastic lid, then remove and place on the table ready to paint.

The 3 colours you have—red, yellow and blue — are the basic primary colours and from these you can mix up the other 4 colours of the rainbow in the jars or lids you have ready:
- blue and yellow make green
- red and yellow make orange
- blue and red make violet
- blue and violet make indigo

Now that the paints are mixed, paint yourself a large rainbow, making sure you have the colours in the right order (from top to bottom, Red, Orange, Yellow, Green, Blue, Indigo, Violet). When finished, carefully fit the cardboard into the tray and put it out in the rain for a few minutes.

Just give it long enough so that the colours flow and blend together, and your rainbow looks like a real one. Take it inside and allow to dry before hanging it.

Reef Knot

What makes a rainbow?

Rainbows are formed when the air is still full of raindrops and the sun comes out. The white light from the sun is really made up of 7 beams of colour — red, orange, yellow, green, blue, indigo and violet. When the white beam hits the raindrops it is bent, and so we have our rainbow.

These 7 colours are referred to as the spectrum — the colours produced when white light is deflected. Each colour has a wavelength — red is the longest and violet is the shortest.

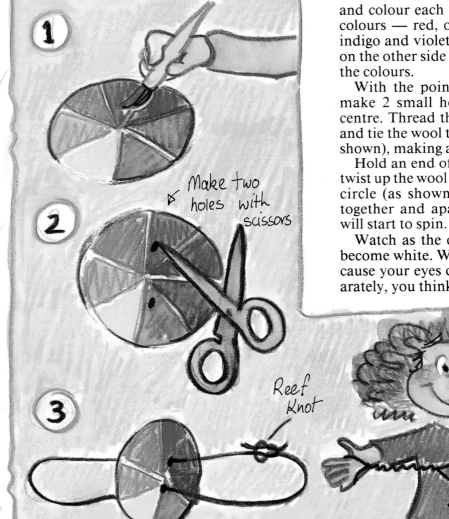

Make two holes with scissors

Reef Knot

TWIRL!!

Disappearing colours

You will need:
- jam-jar lid
- cardboard
- pencil
- ruler
- coloured pencils
- scissors
- length of wool

How to make:
On the cardboard use the jam-jar lid to draw a circle. Divide the circle into 7 equal parts and colour each part in one of the rainbow colours — red, orange, yellow, green, blue, indigo and violet, in that order. Repeat this on the other side of the cardboard, matching the colours.

With the point of the scissors, carefully make 2 small holes on either side of the centre. Thread the wool through both holes and tie the wool together with a reef knot (as shown), making a loop.

Hold an end of the loop in each hand and twist up the wool by spinning your hands in a circle (as shown). Now move your hands together and apart and your colour-wheel will start to spin.

Watch as the colours blend together and become white. What is happening is that because your eyes cannot see each colour separately, you think there are no colours at all.

13

Rainy Day Food

Submarines

A submarine is a special long bread roll oozing lovely fillings. In fact you can fit in more filling by removing some of the soft bread before you begin. They are ideal for snacks in your rainy day den (see page 36).

You will need:
> long bread roll each
> butter, margarine, or
> fancy butter (recipe below)

Suggested fillings:
- finely cut chicken and mayonnaise
- sardines, lemon juice and onions
- crystallised fruit moistened with orange juice
- finely chopped nuts and cream cheese
- peanut butter with raisins and nuts
- grated cheese and mustard or onion
- grated cheese, celery and mayonnaise
- sliced apple, cheese and mayonnaise

How to make:
Slice the rolls lengthways, not quite through. Butter well — don't skimp on the butter because it won't taste nearly as good.

Now pile on the filling of your choice, covering the roll from end to end. Close the top over and wrap in plastic film or foil until you are ready to eat.

Fancy butter

You will need:
> butter or margarine
> basin
> mustard, horseradish, chives, parsley, curry powder, anchovy sauce

How to make:
A half-cup of butter or margarine, which has been creamed (beaten), will spread up to 40 slices of bread, so work out about how much you will need before you begin.

Place the required amount of butter or margarine in the basin, put the basin in the sink and surround it with warm water. It will probably take about 20 minutes for the butter to soften.

Cream the butter, adding whichever condiments you feel will go well with your submarine filling.

Spread the bread rolls while the butter or margarine is still soft as it will spread more evenly.

14

David's toast

You will need:
slice of toast for each
    person
butter or margarine
saucepan
cup chopped cooked meat
diced apple
diced tomato
curry powder
egg

How to make:
Prepare the toast. Carefully melt the butter
in the saucepan over a low heat, making sure
it doesn't burn.

Add the chopped meat, apple, tomato and
curry powder and blend with a little water
into a nice, smooth paste. Stir in the egg.

Spread on the toast. This makes a great
snack for a cold rainy day, especially if
served with the hot chocolate drink which
follows.

Hot chocolate supreme

You will need:
cocoa
milk
marshmallows

How to make:
Follow the directions on the can or package
of cocoa, making up a mug of hot chocolate
for each person. Beat thoroughly until it's
nice and frothy. Now float marshmallows on
the top of each mug. It's yummy!

Jokes and Puzzles

Wet jokes

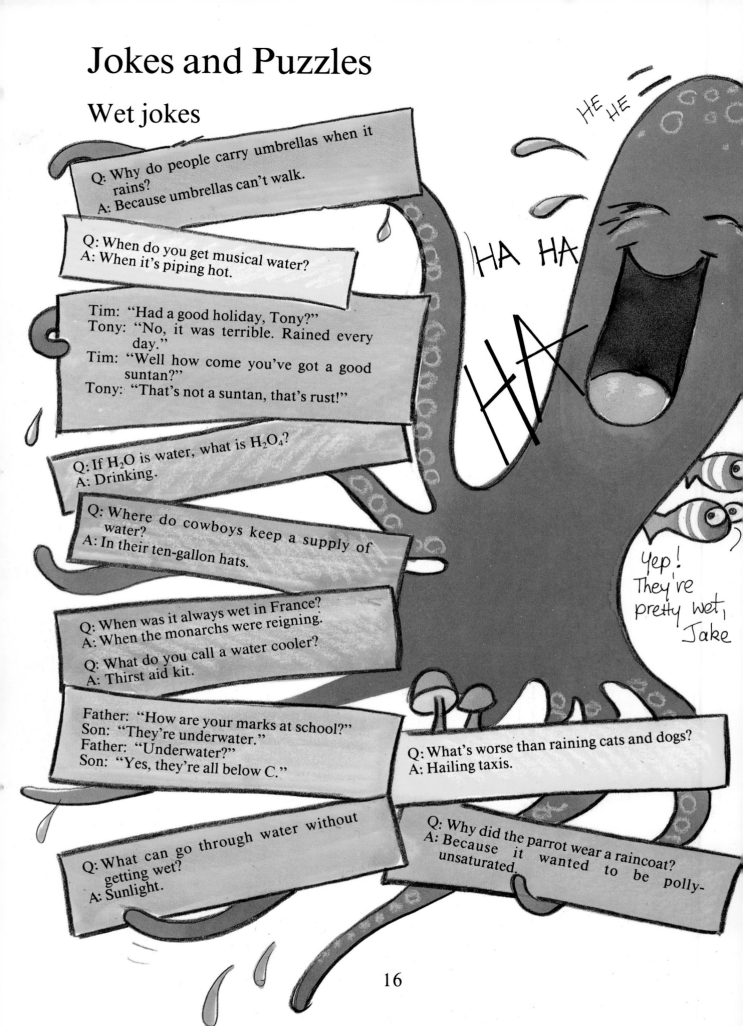

Q: Why do people carry umbrellas when it rains?
A: Because umbrellas can't walk.

Q: When do you get musical water?
A: When it's piping hot.

Tim: "Had a good holiday, Tony?"
Tony: "No, it was terrible. Rained every day."
Tim: "Well how come you've got a good suntan?"
Tony: "That's not a suntan, that's rust!"

Q: If H_2O is water, what is H_2O_4?
A: Drinking.

Q: Where do cowboys keep a supply of water?
A: In their ten-gallon hats.

Q: When was it always wet in France?
A: When the monarchs were reigning.

Q: What do you call a water cooler?
A: Thirst aid kit.

Father: "How are your marks at school?"
Son: "They're underwater."
Father: "Underwater?"
Son: "Yes, they're all below C."

Q: What's worse than raining cats and dogs?
A: Hailing taxis.

Q: What can go through water without getting wet?
A: Sunlight.

Q: Why did the parrot wear a raincoat?
A: Because it wanted to be polly-unsaturated.

HE HE

HA HA

HA

Yep! They're pretty wet, Jake

How many more, Mum?

Watery puzzles

1 Here are 4 tanks. The 2 smaller tanks are half the size of the large tanks. One tenth of 1 of the larger tanks would be filled by 1 bucket full of water. How many buckets of water are needed to fill all the tanks?

(Answer: 30)

2 Here are 3 toy sailing boats, 1 for each child in the family. A child, who has 1 brother and 1 sister, owns 1 of the boats. The second boat is owned by a child who has 2 sisters. Work out how many of the boats in this family are owned by girls and how many by boys.

(Answer: 2 by girls, 1 by a boy)

Much longer, Mate?

3 There is a speedboat race about to start, but 6 of the boats have broken down. If it takes 2 mechanics 2 hours to fix 2 boats, how many mechanics will fix 6 boats in 6 hours?

(Answer: 2)

4 All sorts of things that have something to do with rainy weather have been listed below. These words are hidden in the grid. The words may be written forwards, backwards, horizontally, vertically, or even diagonally. We have circled 1 to give you a start. Now see how many you can find from this list:

RAINCOAT	RAIN	FLOOD	CYCLONE
UMBRELLA	HAIL	STORM	WELLIES
RAINBOW	SNOW	CLOUDS	TYPHOON
WATERFALL	WIND	RIVER	GALOSHES
RAINMAKER	LAKE	WATER	PUDDLES
ICICLES	DAM	WAVES	MUDDY
BLEAK	SHIP	CANOE	BOAT
SHARK	FROST	TIDES	COLD
MUD	STREAM	CREEK	FISH

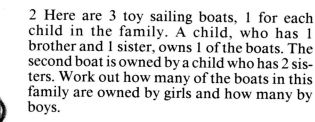

```
L A P G A L O S H E S U
A T H S I F N I P D U M
K E R N O O H P Y T Z B
E O E E W R C R E E K R
P N V A E C O L D O Y E
R A I N M A K E R H I L
L C R O A S H I P A C L
K A E L B T I D E S I A
S D U O L C L I A H C N
K R A H S T O R M M L W
W A T E R F A L L H E A
N L V D O O L F R O S T
T A O B R A I N B O W E
W I N D T A O C N I A R
M A E R T S E L D D U P
Y P C Y C L O N E Z X T
W E L L I E S Y D D U M
```

Blindfold Skills

The games suggested here need at least 3 or more players, so are ideal when you have visitors on a rainy day.

We recommend you use a large brown paper grocery bag, which is placed over the player's head. *Never use plastic.* A large, clean handkerchief, folded and tied behind the head is also a good blindfold.

Catch a thief

You will need:
> blindfold
> tray with various small items
> (pencils, erasers, etc.)
> rolled-up newspaper

How to play:
One player is picked to be the shopkeeper and blindfolded. They sit at a table, with the tray of goodies in front of them, armed with the rolled-up newspaper.

The other players all go to the sides of the room — their base. The object is to sneak up and steal 1 item at a time from the tray and return to base without being hit by the shopkeeper's swatter.

If hit, the player must return to base empty-handed and start again. The winner is the thief with the most loot when the tray is empty. The winner becomes the next shopkeeper.

Right

Wrong

Through the maze

You will need:
> obstacles for course
> blindfold

How to play:
Collect dozens of unbreakable objects like plastic cups, plates and bottles, as well as thread spools, saucepans and so forth.

Blindfold the first player *before* setting up the obstacle course across the room. The idea is for the player to hop across the room being guided by the instructions from the other players.

Keep a score of how many obstacles are knocked over, or pushed out of place. Every player has a turn and the obstacle course is changed each time, as soon as the player is blindfolded. The winner is the one with the lowest score.

Shoes and socks jumble

You will need:
> shoes and socks
> blindfolds for all players

How to play:
All players take off their shoes and socks and jumble them together in a pile in the middle of the room.

Everyone puts on a blindfold and holds hands making a circle around the pile of shoes and socks. Walk in a circle 5 times one way, then 5 times the other.

The players then sit down and someone calls "go". Everyone now tries to find their shoes and socks and put them on.

Draw up your paper like this ↓

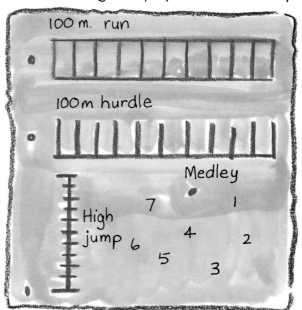

How to play...

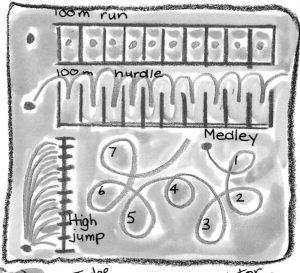

Judge

Spectator

Sports person

Blindfold sports

You will need:
blindfold for each player
pencil and paper for each player

How to play:
All players are blindfolded, except the judge whose job it is to place the players' pencils on the next start mark as they finish each event.

Before putting on the blindfolds each player marks out these track and field events on their paper:

1 The 100 metre run
2 The 100 metre hurdle
3 The high jump
4 The medley

1 The 100 metre run
Place pencil on starting block. The object is to place 1 dot in each square. Score by counting 1 point for each square that contains 1 dot.

2 The 100 metre hurdle
Place pencil on start. Draw 10 continuous arches as you leap over the hurdles. Score 1 point for each hurdle cleared. No score if your jump is not between the top and bottom of the hurdle, or if you have 2 goes at a hurdle.

3 The high jump
Place pencil on start. You have 10 heights to clear beginning with number 1. Score 1 point for each successful jump. No score if you jump the same height more than once, or if you don't clear the jumps clearly.

4 The medley
This one is hard. Place pencil on start. The idea is to travel around each number, in the correct order, circling each one as you go. Score 2 for each successful circle.

19

Musical Noise

A rainy day is the ideal time to set up your own pop group. Start by making your musical instruments; decide what you will play; practise; then invite your family in for a pop concert!

Chimes

You will need:
    8 glass bottles same size and shape
      (juice bottles are ideal)
    ruler
    felt-tip pen
    water (in a jug or kettle)
    wooden spoon

How to make:
Place the 8 bottles in a straight line on a table, making sure they are close together but not touching. With the ruler measure up from the bottom of each bottle, drawing a line with the felt-tip pen as follows:

    20 mm (¾ in) up on 1st bottle
    40 mm (1½ in) up on 2nd bottle

and so on. Now take the jug or kettle of water and fill each bottle to the line you have marked (as shown).

Your chimes are ready to play. Take the wooden spoon and tap each bottle below the water line. Listen to the notes getting higher, or lower, depending on the amount of water in the bottle.

Bells

You will need:
    5 bottle tops
    length wood 30 cm x 2 cm (12 in x ¾ in)
      or old wooden ruler
    hammer
    5 small nails

How to make:
Attach the bottle tops to the flat side of the wood with the small nails. The secret is not to hammer them on too tightly or they won't rattle. Also, make certain that the bottle tops are just touching each other.

Drums

You will need:
    ice-cream container (with lid)
    string for neck strap
    scissors

How to make:
First, make certain that the ice-cream container is really clean, otherwise you'll get very sticky! Next, ask someone to help you make 2 holes in the opposite sides of the container, using the scissors (as shown), just below where the lid fits on.

Take the string and measure the right length from 1 hole, up round your neck and down to the other hole. Tie off both ends through the holes using a figure-of-eight knot (as shown). Fit lid firmly in place.

Juice bottles are best!

Bottle tops

Wooden ruler

Nail tops on loosely!

Ask an adult to help!

20

Drumsticks

You will need:
- scissors
- coloured paper
- 2 dowel sticks 30 cm (12 in) long
- 2 thumb tacks

How to make:
Cut coloured paper into equal lengths of about 50 cm long by 1 cm wide (20 in x ⅓ in). Firmly attach about 5 lengths to one end of each dowel stick with thumb tack (as shown). Your drum set is now complete.

Lid

Figure of eight knot

Drumsticks

Decorations

Decorate all the instruments you have made by using felt-tip pens or water-colour paints. It will certainly brighten up your pop group!

Rattles

You will need:
- plastic bottle
  (soft drink is best)
- rice, macaroni or small stones

How to make:
Wash the bottle thoroughly, then dry both inside and out. Pour in a handful of rice or macaroni or small stones and screw the lid on tightly. Hey presto! One rattle!

Extras

If you don't have enough instruments for all the members of your pop group, borrow the following from the kitchen cupboards:

♪ 2 saucepan lids, banged together, make a great set of cymbals

♪ a frying pan tapped with a fork can give a good rhythm

♪ a cheese-grater tied to a piece of string and played with a teaspoon adds an interesting sound

♪ various sizes of empty bottles — which one of your group can blow across — add extra notes.

Water Fun

Blowing bubbles

You will need:
> soap powder or detergent
> hot water
> sugar
> thin wire (fuse or copper wire)
> pliers

How to make:

First make up your bubble solution by mixing 6 tablespoons of soap powder, or detergent, into a cup of hot water. Leave this mixture to stand for an hour or more, then stir in 1 tablespoon of sugar (this makes the bubbles stronger).

Remember, because the bubbles have sugar in them they will leave a sticky mark where they burst, so do your bubble blowing in the bathroom where it's easier to clean up!

While waiting for your bubble solution to cool and settle, make a selection of different-shaped bubble blowers, using the thin wire and pliers. Try these shapes:

Make sure all your shapes are fully closed loops otherwise the bubble blower won't work (as shown).

Always leave yourself a piece of wire long enough to use as a handle.

The bubble solution should not be frothy; if it is, leave it stand until flat. Always push your bubble blower into the solution slowly.

You can blow enormous bubbles by dipping your hands into the bubble solution and, either make a circle with your thumb and first finger, or place your little fingers and the base of your hands together then open to make a blowing circle.

These will work!

This one won't work

Matchstick magic

You will need:
> 6 used wooden matches
> clean bowl of water
> sugar cube
> bar of soap
> drinking straw

How to make:

Float the matches on the surface of the water (as shown). Carefully place the sugar cube in the centre of the bowl. The matches will slowly move towards the sugar because it is absorbing the water.

Remove the sugar, the matches, and throw away the water.

Start again with a clean bowl of water. Float the matches as before. This time push a lump of soap on to the end of the drinking straw, making sure it is firmly attached. Lower this into the centre of the bowl so that only the soap is touching the surface of the water (as shown).

This time the matches will move towards the edge of the bowl. This is because the surface of the water has a skin, in which the soap has made a hole. The breaking of the surface tension of this skin causes the matches to move away as the skin moves away.

Soap w
make the
matches mo
outwards

Floating needle

You will need:
>   needle
>   fork
>   clean bowl of water

How it works:
This will also show you how the skin on the surface of the water works, and gives you some idea of just how strong it is.

Place the needle on the prongs of the fork (as shown). Now slowly lower this into the bowl of clean water. Take your time. You must allow the skin, which has been broken by the fork, time to form again under the needle and hold it up. The needle should now be floating on the surface of the water.

Remember not to attempt to remove the fork, leave it in the dish or you'll ruin your trick.

Water magic

You will need:
>   2 glass bottles (exactly the same)
>   water
>   salt
>   food colouring
>   piece of cardboard

How to make:
Check that the bottles are exactly the same size otherwise this trick won't work. They also need to be thoroughly clean. Ask a friend to help because you'll need an extra pair of hands.

Fill both bottles with water. Add at least 4 tablespoons of salt to 1 bottle and mix thoroughly, making sure all the salt is dissolved before you begin.

Into the second bottle add several drops of food colouring. Again, mix well and make a good strong colour.

Place a square of cardboard on the top of the bottle containing the salty water. Now hold the card tightly as you turn the bottle upside down and place it on the other bottle (as shown). Carefully slide out the piece of cardboard.

Now watch as the waters change place. The salty water in the top bottle will slowly go into the bottom bottle, while the coloured water will rise from the bottom to the top bottle.

This all happens because the salty water is much denser and will always sink to the bottom.

Salt water

Pull out carefully

Coloured water

23

Indoor Games

A smelly game

You will need:

    smelly things like coffee, onion, curry powder, cloves
    pieces of material 12 cm (4¾ in) square
    elastic bands or string
    long piece of string
    clothes pegs

How to make:

Ask an adult to help you set this one up — especially when choosing the things to smell because you don't want to use something like pepper, that can burn the inside of the nose if any of the players sniff too hard.

Place each item on a separate piece of material, fold the corners diagonally across to close, and secure with an elastic band or a piece of string (as shown).

Stretch a line across the room and, using the clothes pegs, attach each bag at nose level. Now ask your friends to try and identify what's in each bag. They can only sniff — no touching or squeezing.

Blow ball

You will need:

    chair for each player
    ping pong ball
    clear table

How to play:

You can play this game with as few as 2 players, but the more the merrier.

All players sit on a chair, hands behind their backs. The ping pong ball is placed in the centre of the table.

The object of the game is to blow the ball over the edge of the table opposite you. A goal is scored each time a player succeeds.

Sardines

You will need:

    4 or more players

How to play:

This is a great inside hiding game for a rainy

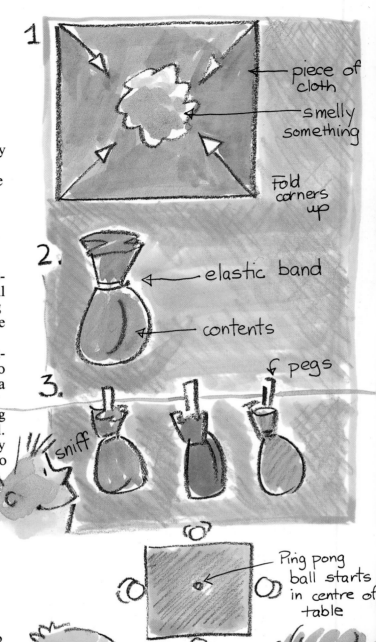

1   piece of cloth

smelly something

Fold corners up

2.   elastic band

contents

3.   pegs

sniff

Ping pong ball starts in centre of table

hands behind backs

day, but check with the adults that it's O.K.; in fact, they may want to join in.

One player is chosen to go and hide somewhere in the house, while all the other players stay together, slowly counting to 100.

Then everyone sets off in different directions to find the first player. When someone finds him they squash into the hiding place too. And so it goes on until all the players are packed into the hiding place like sardines.

The player who was first to find the hiding place is the next person to go and hide.

Alphabet scavenge

You will need:
    3 or more players

How to play:
This is an indoor scavenger hunt that can be played in teams if you have enough friends visiting.

The object is for the players to find items in the house that begin with the 26 letters of the alphabet. For example:
    A — apple, animal
    B — book, bread, beans
    C — cake, cup, cat

If you are short of time then reduce the list to about 20 letters, cutting out the more difficult ones like Q, Y and Z.

Paper fashions

HELP!

You will need:
    plenty of old newspaper
    sticky tape

How to make:
Take turns to dress up each player, or divide into pairs and work as a team. You can do this alone if there's no one there to play with.

The idea is to create the craziest gear possible, using only the newspaper, with the sticky tape to hold it together. At the end the only parts of the player left visible should be the face, hands and feet.

Ask an adult to be the judge.

Paper and Plastic Models

Try these simple flying models. They don't take long to build; the materials will be easy to find; and they are all on a small scale so that you can fly them inside and not cause any problems.

1. Fold through centre

2. Fold in corners

3. Fold in again

Chuck glider

You will need:
sheet of 8½″ × 11″ writing paper
pencil
ruler

How to make:
The paper must not be too light — we suggest a sheet of good quality writing paper. Crease all folds by using the ruler, and always match each corner exactly.

Step 1 — Fold the paper in half lengthways.
Step 2 — Fold in left-hand corners.
Step 3 — Again fold from the left.
Step 4 — Close up (as shown). The next 2 folds are outwards.
Step 5 — Turn up tail. Don't crease the tail as it can be adjusted for different flight patterns.

4. Close up then fold wings outward

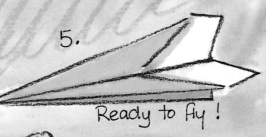

5. Ready to fly!

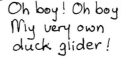

Oh boy! Oh boy! My very own duck glider!

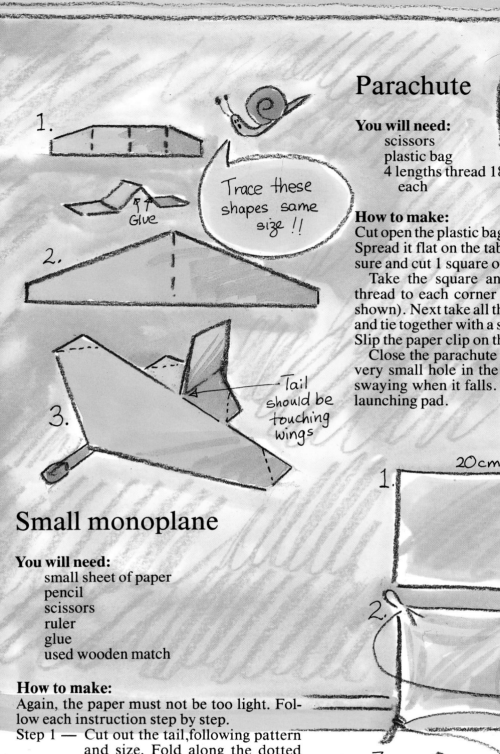

1.

Glue

2.

3.

Trace these shapes same size !!

Tail should be touching wings

Parachute

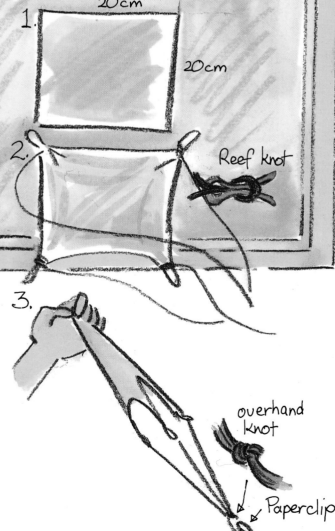

Tiny hole

Plastic bags can be dangerous. Ask an adult to help!

You will need:
    scissors
    plastic bag
    4 lengths thread 18 cm (7 in)
      each

How to make:
Cut open the plastic bag following the seams. Spread it flat on the table and carefully measure and cut 1 square of 20 cm (8 in).

    Take the square and attach a length of thread to each corner using a reef knot (as shown). Next take all the loose ends of thread and tie together with a simple overhand knot. Slip the paper clip on this end.

    Close the parachute (as shown) and clip a very small hole in the top. This will stop it swaying when it falls. Now find a nice high launching pad.

1.

20cm

20cm

2.

Reef knot

3.

overhand knot

Paperclip

Small monoplane

You will need:
    small sheet of paper
    pencil
    scissors
    ruler
    glue
    used wooden match

How to make:
Again, the paper must not be too light. Follow each instruction step by step.

Step 1 — Cut out the tail, following pattern and size. Fold along the dotted lines and glue together.

Step 2 — Cut out the wings, again the same size and pattern as here.

Step 3 — Glue the wings to the match and glue the tail so that it touches the back of the wing (as shown).

Step 4 — Wait for the glue to dry thoroughly before bending the tips up at an angle.

be late

ur flight . . .

e are they?

Charades

Charades is the ideal game for a rainy day when you have several friends visiting because it offers hours of fun.

Choose a player who will be the "actor". From now on they cannot say a word, but must communicate only by mime.

The actor thinks of a book title, a film, a TV show, or a song. So that the other players know what they are looking for, the actor indicates which category they have chosen by the following means:

book title — both hands held palms upward to show an open book

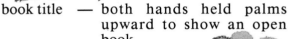

film title — mime winding a handle to indicate a movie camera

song title — hold a make-believe microphone and pretend to sing

TV show — draw a box in the air

Next, the number of words in the title to be guessed is indicated by holding up the appropriate number of fingers.

The position of a word in the title is also shown in the same way. You don't have to do the words in the right order, a word that is difficult to act out can usually be guessed by the players once they have worked out the other words in the title.

A small word is shown by holding the thumb and first finger close together. For a long word the actor stretches their arms wide apart.

Long words are best if broken into syllables. The first syllable is shown by holding 1 finger against the forearm, the second syllable by holding 2 fingers, and so on.

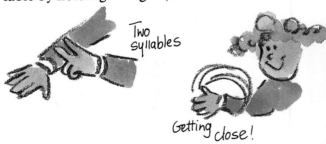

The actor is allowed to help the players in many ways, but they must never speak. For example, if the players are getting close to the answer, the actor makes a circular movement with their hand to encourage the players to keep guessing along those lines.

28

Some words are hard for the actor to portray, so another way is to indicate that the word "sounds" like something else. To show this the actor will cup their hand behind their ear, and act out the word with the rhyming sound.

Here's an example of a song title: 'Silent Night'.

"It's a song title"

"Getting close? Silent?"

"Silent fight?"

"With 2 words"

"Now... 2nd word"

"Close... Fight? Bright?"

"The first word"

"Sounds like..."

Yes!

"NIGHT?"

"Hush? Quiet?"

"Box? Fight?"

"SILENT NIGHT!"

Rainy Day Gardening

Ask if you can borrow the garage, porch or balcony to work in, and put on your raincoat and boots before leaving the house.

Rainy days are great times for creating something different, so why not plant an old-fashioned flower garden or a herb garden. Both of these can be planted in something portable that can be brought inside to be enjoyed by everyone.

The container

Ask an adult to help!

You will need:

    hammer and nail
    large garden-pot saucer (plastic)
        or old garbage can lid
    pebbles
    light potting soil

How to make:

Begin by hammering drainage holes through the base of either the garden-pot saucer or old garbage can lid.

Use the pebbles to spread over the bottom of the container. These stop your soil from becoming too heavy by providing drainage.

Now shake in the potting mixture, making sure that it goes down through the pebbles and fills up all the gaps. You are now ready to begin planting.

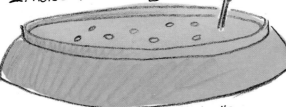
1. Holes for drainage

2. Spread pebbles over bottom

3. Fill with potting mixture

Planting guide

Plants:

If planting small plants, use a dibber to make the hole (this is a special gardening tool, but a pencil will do just as well). Firm the soil well around the plant and remember to keep it watered after the rain has stopped.

yum!

Seeds:

When planting seeds, use the dibber to make a trough about 1 cm ($\frac{1}{3}$ in) deep. Carefully place the seeds in the trough (check instructions on packet for how far apart they should be), then gently sprinkle soil on the top. Smooth out and keep watered.

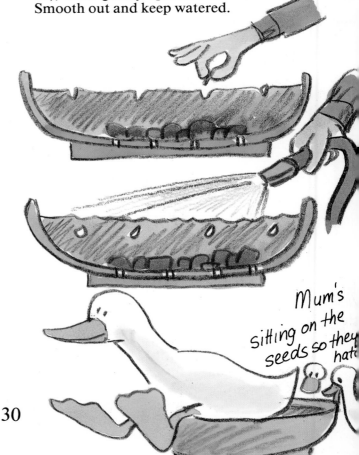

Mum's sitting on the seeds so they hat

30

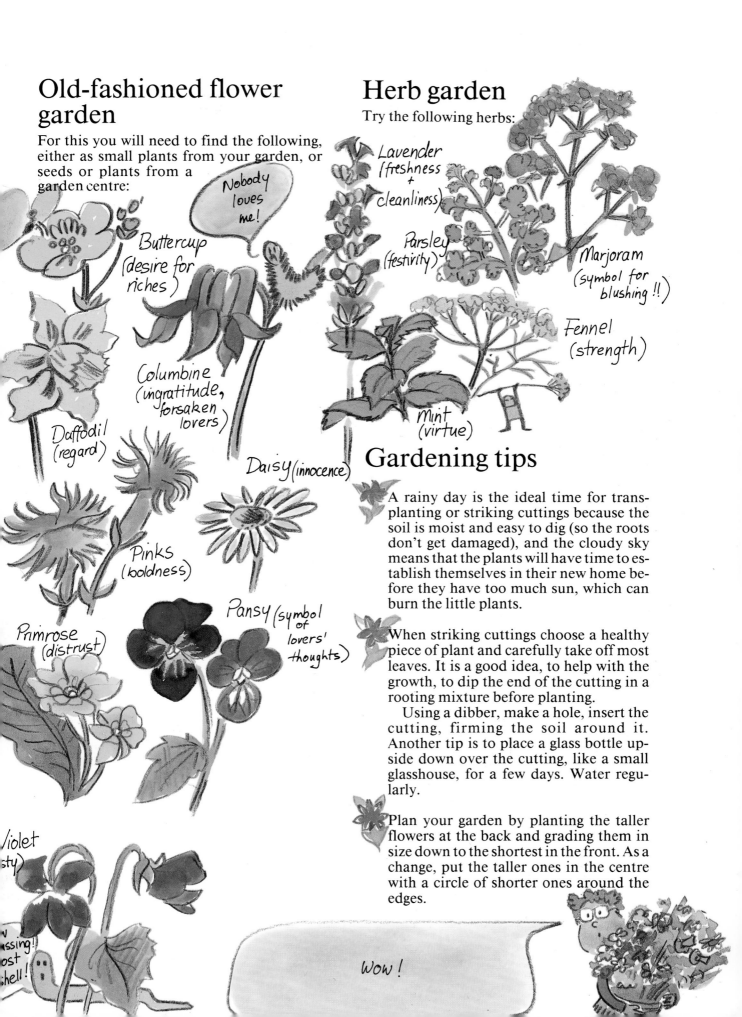

Old-fashioned flower garden

For this you will need to find the following, either as small plants from your garden, or seeds or plants from a garden centre:

Buttercup (desire for riches)

Nobody loves me!

Columbine (ingratitude, forsaken lovers)

Daffodil (regard)

Daisy (innocence)

Pinks (boldness)

Primrose (distrust)

Pansy (symbol of lovers' thoughts)

Violet ...ty)

...sing! ...ost ...hell!

Herb garden

Try the following herbs:

Lavender (freshness + cleanliness)

Parsley (festivity)

Marjoram (symbol for blushing !!)

Fennel (strength)

Mint (virtue)

Gardening tips

A rainy day is the ideal time for transplanting or striking cuttings because the soil is moist and easy to dig (so the roots don't get damaged), and the cloudy sky means that the plants will have time to establish themselves in their new home before they have too much sun, which can burn the little plants.

When striking cuttings choose a healthy piece of plant and carefully take off most leaves. It is a good idea, to help with the growth, to dip the end of the cutting in a rooting mixture before planting.

Using a dibber, make a hole, insert the cutting, firming the soil around it. Another tip is to place a glass bottle upside down over the cutting, like a small glasshouse, for a few days. Water regularly.

Plan your garden by planting the taller flowers at the back and grading them in size down to the shortest in the front. As a change, put the taller ones in the centre with a circle of shorter ones around the edges.

Wow !

When the Rain Stops

As soon as the rain has stopped, go into the garden and check on the experiments you set up before the rain started.

The most important job of all is to release the small creatures you have caught in the glass jar (see page 11). Your next stop should be the rain gauge. Record the fall in a notebook and don't forget to empty the rainwater out before setting it up again (see page 10).

The next job is to look at the various plastic cups set up around the garden and see how unevenly the rain has fallen. Again, record it all in your notebook (see page 11).

There will probably be a number of puddles about so, to see how full they are of all kinds of foreign matter, try this simple experiment:

A water filter

You will need:
> plastic bottle
> ruler
> scissors
> coffee-filter paper
>   (or blotting paper)
> wet sand
> puddle water

How to make:
Measure 10 cm (4 in) down the plastic bottle and, using the scissors, carefully cut off the top. Remove the cap, it's not needed. Turn this top section upside down into the bottom half of the bottle (as shown).

Into this funnel place the coffee-filter paper (or blotting paper), then add the wet sand. Now pour some puddle water in and watch it drip through into the bottle. It will be much cleaner than the water you poured in.

You can improve your filter system by adding some crushed charcoal on top of the sand, with another layer of sand on top of that.

DO NOT DRINK THE WATER — you have filtered out the dirt, but not the germs.

32

A coloured fountain

You will need:
- glass screw-top bottle
- hammer and nail
- drinking straw
- cold and hot water
- food colouring
- plasticine
- needle
- bucket

How to make:

Unscrew the cap from the bottle. Using the hammer and nail make a hole in the cap big enough for the drinking straw to slip in. Ask an adult to help if you find this difficult.

Half fill the bottle with cold water, then add several drops of food colouring so that the water turns a good strong colour. Screw the cap on tightly and push the straw through so that the end is well below the level of the water.

Use the plasticine to seal around the hole where the straw comes out of the cap and plug the top of the straw with a ball of plasticine. Use the needle to make a thin hole through the plug into the straw (as shown).

Place the bottle in a bucket (the bucket must be deep enough to contain the whole bottle). Fill the bucket with hot water.

Your fountain will now begin to spurt as the coloured water rises up through the straw and out of the tiny hole.

Warning:

After a lot of rain the small streams, storm-water channels and drainage ditches, which carry the excess water away, will be very full and flowing swiftly. DO NOT PLAY NEAR THEM — you could be swept away.

Mud!

When the rain has stopped get into some *very* old clothes and boots and set out to explore what the world is like after rain. You'll be surprised at what you find and the fun you can have.

Mud masterpiece

You will need:
- squishy mud
- water
- old spoon
- thick cardboard
- old paintbrush
- old comb

How to make:
Find a clear space near a good supply of nice squishy mud. Add more water if too thick and mix up well, using your hands, until the mixture is the right thickness.

Spoon some mud onto the cardboard. Using the old paintbrush begin your mud masterpiece. Keep adding mud as needed. Use your fingers (pretend you are finger painting), the old comb, or anything else that will make an interesting pattern. Look around for stones, feathers, leaves, sticks, or anything to add to this marvellous painting.

When finished, carefully carry it inside to dry, or if the sun is shining leave it outside.

Mud monster

You will need:
- squishy mud
- bucket or saucepan
- spade or spoon

How to make:
This mixture of mud needs to be drier than the lot you used for painting your masterpiece. If the mud is too squishy hunt around for some drier dirt (try under a big tree, or near the house), then add this to the mud until the mixture becomes stiffer.

Now it's over to your imagination to create the craziest monster you can think of. Use your hands to shape the basic body structure, then use the bucket, saucepan or spade for special shapes and curves.

Add stones, sticks, leaves, or whatever comes to hand from around the garden. Why not build a whole family of mud monsters and leave them to dry in the sun?

Mud prints

You will need:
- squishy mud
- bucket or saucepan
- spade or spoon
- collection of old shoes

How to make:
You will need a nice long stretch of squishy mud for this one. Mix up the mud in your bucket or saucepan and spread it along the ground for about 2 metres (6½ feet). It will need to be about 2 cm (¾ in) thick.

Now put on 1 old sneaker and 1 lady's high-heel shoe and walk along your mud road. Next, try a boot and an old sandal. Take giant steps, then small steps. You can always smooth out the mud and start again. Great fun!

1 — Weigh the mud — Kitchen scales

2 — Heat the mud slowly

3 — Weigh again (when cool)

Mud experiment

You will need:
- squishy mud
- saucepan
- scales
- spoon

How to make:
Half fill the saucepan with good squishy mud. Take it inside and ask an adult if you can use the scales and the stove.

Weigh the mud, then place the saucepan on the stove and heat it slowly, stirring occasionally. As the mud begins to heat, steam will rise — this is the water evaporating.

Your mixture will gradually dry out. Turn off the stove and, when the saucepan is cool, weigh it again and see how much weight it has lost.

Rainy Day Dens

Dens are fun to build and great to play in when finished. Here are a few ideas for indoor and outdoor dens to build on a rainy day.

Indoor dens

These can be built in all sorts of places using things from around the house like furniture, old blankets or sheets, and pillows. Decide where you will build and what you will use, then let your imagination go and see what happens.

Remember to check with an adult before you begin. Then try a few of these ideas:

Two-chair den

I always knew we'd find a use for those encyclopaedias!

Big

Dining table den

Bed den

Use pegs or big clips

Double-decker den

Children... where are you?

If chairs are too wobbly try a pile of pillows...

Outdoor dens

If it's a day of light rain with very little wind, then it's fun to build your own outdoor waterproof den. Try these:

Umbrella dens

Umbrella den
First ask if you can borrow all the umbrellas in the house — you will need at least 5. Take these outside and carefully arrange them so that they form a waterproof shelter (as shown). One umbrella can be the door that rolls aside letting you and your friends crawl in and out.

Wear old clothes and take a groundsheet or raincoat to sit on.

Arab tent
For this den you will need a large umbrella — a golfing umbrella is best, but any large one will do. You will also need an old groundsheet, or piece of large plastic, or an old raincoat, and lots of safety pins.

Open the umbrella and attach the groundsheet (or plastic) to the ribs of the umbrella with the safety pins, taking care not to damage the fabric.

This den can be used on its side (as shown), but it is much better if you can stand it straight up using a few bricks to hold it in place (as shown).

Remember to take something waterproof to sit on.

Boats

While it's raining make some of these small boats ready to sail in the puddles when the rain has stopped.

Styrofoam boats

These are light and float extremely well. Find a styrofoam tray like the ones that you see at the vegetable store or supermarket. Using a bread knife, carefully cut several different shapes and sizes (number 1, below).

Try these:
Find a thin stick for the masts. A piece of dowel is ideal but pencils can be used, or if it's a very small boat a wooden match will work (this will push straight into the styrofoam and stay firm).

Next, cut out various sail shapes and sticky tape or thread onto the mast. Try these sail styles (see number 2, below).

Any shape will do!

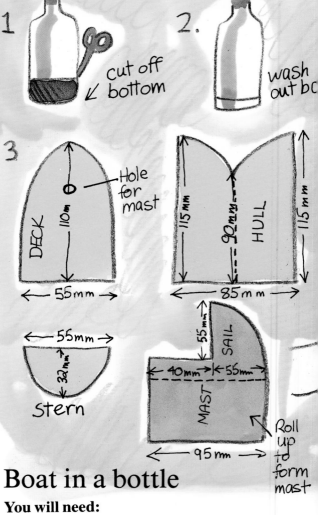

Boat in a bottle

You will need:
   plastic soft-drink bottle
   scissors and ruler
   pencil
   heavy paper or light cardboard
   regular transparent sticky tape
   heavy, coloured tape
   plasticine
   glue

Ask an adult to help!

How to make:
Measuring approximately 2.5 cm (1 in) from the base of your plastic bottle, draw an even line around the bottle with a felt-tip pen.

With scissors, make a small hole or slit in the plastic (enough to be able to start cutting) and cutting along the line you drew, remove base. Remember, this base has to be put back onto the bottle, so be careful. Now you can wash out the bottle.

Following the patterns shown, measure and draw the parts of your boat onto the paper or cardboard. Cut out each section.

Take the hull and carefully fold it along the centre dotted line. Join the curved edges together with sticky tape.

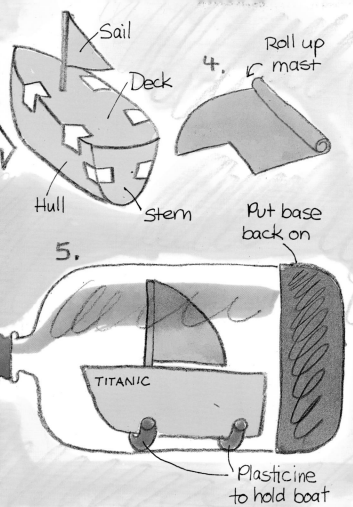

Sail

Deck

4.

Roll up mast

Hull

Stern

Put base back on

5.

TITANIC

Plasticine to hold boat

Carefully fit the stern in place and secure with sticky tape. The deck is next, but before it is fitted, make the hole for the mast. Put the deck in place with sticky tape.

Tightly roll the mast from the edge (as shown), as far as the dotted line. Fasten with sticky tape and push into the hole in the deck.

Paint your boat using water-colours or felt-tip pens. Add a name on the stern, and a design and number on the sail.

While the paint is drying, make the stand. Roll 2 pieces of plasticine to 3 cm long by 1 cm high (1¼ × ⅓ in) and make a "V" shape in the middle of each (as shown). This is where the hull will sit.

Place these 2 stands in the centre of the bottle, about 7 cm (2¾ in) apart. Press them firmly onto the bottle. Next, gently place your boat on the stand, making sure that it is held firmly in place by the plasticine.

Now, position the base back onto the bottle and seal with the coloured tape. To make sure it's put on firmly you could put some sticky tape on first, or dabs of quick setting glue. To finish off the design, colour the cap of the bottle the same colour as the tape you used.

Mark's paddle-wheeler

You will need:
> piece soft wood 200 x 120 x 10 mm (8 x 4¾ x ⅓ in)
> thin piece of wood 40 x 100 x 1 mm (1½ x 4 x 1⁄25 in)
> pencil and ruler
> saw
> strong rubber bands

How to make:
On the large block of wood, measure out the boat shape (following the pattern) and rule the lines. With the help of a friend, carefully saw along these lines.

The small notches, that the rubber band fits in, will be difficult, so ask an adult to help if you can't manage them.

Stretch the rubber band over the notches and slip the paddle-wheel in between. Twist the rubber band, hold it while you place your boat in the water — then let it go.

Remember, the tighter the twist in the rubber band the faster your paddle-wheeler will go. Always have a supply of rubber bands.

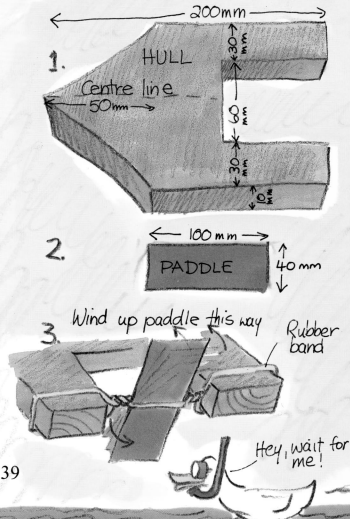

← 200mm →

1. HULL
Centre line
← 50mm →
30 mm
60 mm
30 mm
10 mm

2. ← 100 mm →
PADDLE
40 mm

3. Wind up paddle this way
Rubber band

Move over slow coach

Hey, wait for me!

Typhoon Maze

Find your way to the safety of the eye of the storm.

Watery Disasters

The 4 elements of Nature — earth, air, fire and water — have, over thousands of years, wreaked havoc, at times even changing the face of the land itself. Sometimes, 2 or more of these elements will join together and let loose incredible destruction.

Typhoons, hurricanes and cyclones

These are huge storms, combining the elements of air and water, which form in the seas near the Equator. They are tight, low-pressure zones bringing torrential rains and violent winds that can reach up to 300 km/h (190 mph).

These whirling storms of destruction revolve in an anti-clockwise direction in the Northern Hemisphere and a clockwise spiral in the Southern Hemisphere.
- In the Atlantic they are called hurricanes.
- In the North Pacific they are called typhoons.
- In the Indian Ocean and Australia they are called cyclones.

These storms can last up to 10 days before they become an ordinary rain-bearing depression. At its height, one of these storms can release as much energy every minute as an H-bomb.

Acid rain

Rain is slightly acid even in unpolluted air. The carbon dioxide and other naturally produced acid gases in the air are dissolved by the rain.

Nowadays, rain that falls in North America and Europe is sometimes more acid than lemon juice. Many scientists believe it is formed as a result of burning fossil fuels — such as coal and oil — which are used in industrialised countries.

These fossil fuels produce carbon dioxide, plus small amounts of nitrogen and sulphur dioxide. When these gases mix with the rain in the atmosphere they form a weak solution of nitric acid and sulphuric acid.

Acid rain is one of the factors responsible for turning Canadian and Scandinavian lakes acid and for damaging forest areas, especially in Germany.

Geochemists are now finding evidence that acid rain may have been responsible for helping to wipe out the dinosaurs.
A giant meteorite struck the earth 65 million years ago. Fumes from the impact dissolved to form clouds and the rain caused was as corrosive as battery acid.

World's worst water disasters

Date	Death	Cause	Place
1228	100,000	Flood	Friesland, Netherlands
1642	300,000	Flood	Huang He River, China
1876	215,000	Tsunamis	Bay of Bengal, India
1881	300,000	Typhoon	Haiphong, Vietnam
1887	900,000	Flood	Henan, China
1911	100,000	Flood	Chang Jiang River, China
1939	1,000,000	Flood	Henan, China
1970	500,000	Typhoon/Flood	Bangladesh

Tsunamis terror

Tsunamis are commonly called tidal waves, but they have nothing to do with tides and are usually started by underwater earthquakes.

The word Tsunamis comes from several Japanese words and means "overflowing water". They mostly occur in the Pacific Ocean because so many volcanoes surround its basin.

After an underwater earthquake, the Tsunamis rushes away through the sea. As it nears the coast the water there is sucked out to meet it, leaving any boats in harbours high and dry. Then suddenly it comes, a great wave of destruction, crashing onto the land and travelling inland for great distances.

A few more facts

The first gale warning was issued in 1861.

The word for typhoon is very similar in several eastern languages. In Polynesian, the god of storms is called "Taafuna". In Chinese, a violent rain storm is a "Tyfong", while in Arabic, a whirlwind is known as a "Tyfoon".

Whirlwinds, water spouts and willy willies have been known to carry dust, fish, frogs and various other objects, high into the air before depositing them a long way off.

The Marianas Trench in the Pacific Ocean is the deepest in the world. It has been measured as being 11.03 kilometres (6.85 miles) deep.

In 1880 in Delhi, India, there was a hailstorm which killed 250 people. Many were buried alive under drifts of ice that froze solid.

Rainy Day Folklore

Nowadays weather forecasting is a highly technical business, with satellites giving up-to-the-minute pictures of cloud formations anywhere in the world.

For hundreds of years before these modern inventions, people looked to Nature to provide them with the day's forecast. By being observant, people learned to recognize the signs and predict the weather.

Many of these observations are still with us today in the forms of sayings or folklore. They are still a reliable way of predicting the weather. Why don't you check a few of these out and see how accurate they are?

Weather sayings

Red sky at night, sailor's delight, Red sky in the morning, sailor's take warning.

Swallows flying high means no rain in the sky, Swallows near the ground means rain will come around.

When clouds appear like rocks and towers, The earth's refreshed by frequent showers.

Kill a bug by mistake and the rain will fall. But bury that little bug and the sun will shine.

If you find a frog that looks pale yellow, the weather is going to be fine. However, if it's going to be wet, that same frog will turn a greeny-brown colour within hours.

If you hear a cock crowing long before dawn, it will be a wet day.

Weather hints

A low sunset	— fair weather
A high sunset	— rain and/or wind
Grey sky in the morning	— fine weather
Bright yellow sunset	— wind
Pale yellow sunset	— rain
Red sunset	— fair weather
Dark blue sky	— wind
Light blue sky	— fine weather

When sea birds fly out early in the morning and head for the sea, it means fair weather with light winds.

When sea birds remain over land or fly inland, it means stormy weather is on the way.

Weather superstitions

Thunder turns milk sour
In the days before milk was pasteurised and kept in refrigerators, many people believed that a thunderstorm turned their milk sour. What really happened was that the humid weather curdled the milk.

Whistling up a gale
Superstitious sailors believed that whistling on board their sailing ship would magically start a gale. This was because whistling sounded very like a gale blowing through the rigging.

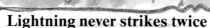

Raining cats and dogs
There are many explanations for this old saying. One goes back to 17th century England at a time when thousands of cats and dogs ran wild in that country. After a heavy storm many of these animals would be found dead and floating down the streets. Some superstitious people assumed they had come down with the rain and been killed when they hit the ground.

Lightning never strikes twice
Since the beginning of time, lightning has frightened people. It has been referred to as "a bolt from heaven", and many myths and legends have been created around it.

One of these myths is that lightning never strikes twice in the same spot, but it is a proven fact that many of the world's tallest buildings, like the C.N. Tower in Toronto, have been struck many times.

Surviving a Rainy Day

We have gathered these tricks and experiments together so that at the end of a long, wet day, you can still find something to do — even though your friends have gone home and everyone in your family has their nose in a book or is watching TV.

A magic glass

We suggest you practise this trick over the sink until you become an expert.

Find a glass with a smooth rim, and an old postcard or a piece of cardboard that size. Fill the glass with water, making sure you wet the rim. Place the postcard across the top of the glass.

Holding the postcard firmly in place, and keeping your hand flat, turn the glass upside down. Slowly move your hand away. The water should stay in the glass, but don't give up if it doesn't. Try again, but stay over the sink.

Colour change

Here is an experiment that shows how water is absorbed and distributed to all parts of a plant.

Fill a vase with water, then colour this water with a strong mixture of food dye. Find a light-coloured flower (white is ideal for this experiment), and place it in the vase.

Next morning check what has happened. You will find that the flower has started to take on the colour of the dye. If you look carefully you may be able to see the coloured water travelling through the tiny veins.

A dry tissue

All you need for this experiment is a bowl of water, a glass and a couple of tissues.

Screw the tissues into a ball and fit them into the bottom of the glass. Turn the glass upside down and place it straight down in the bowl of water. The air in the glass actually forms a barrier against the water and so the tissues will stay dry.

46

Making rain

This experiment shows how water escapes from plants into the atmosphere where it eventually may end up in storm clouds.

Borrow a pot plant for a couple of days and place it on the window sill in your bedroom.

Carefully tie a plastic bag over the whole plant, completely enclosing it, and making a tight seal around the pot (as shown).

After 24 hours you will notice water drops collecting on the inside of the plastic bag. This water has evaporated from the tiny pores in the plant's leaves.

Clear bag

Plant

Tight seal

...stic ...s can be ...erous. Ask ...adult to ...elp you!

Puddle prints

You will need:
- muddy puddle
- piece of white cardboard
- felt-tip pen
- scissors
- clear plastic wrap or film.

How to make:

Stir up a good, sloppy, muddy mixture in a puddle (or an old basin). Place the sheet of white cardboard on a firm, flat surface.

Put your hand into the muddy mixture — making sure that the palm and the fingers are all well-coated with mud — then press onto the cardboard. Try to get a good, clear print.

Allow this to dry in the sun, then carefully mark around the outline with the felt-tip pen. Cut out your handprint and cover with the clear plastic wrap or film

You can also make prints of your feet, or even your dog's paw (if you are gentle).

Now, which one's mine?

A wet trick

This is a fun trick. Find 2 paper cups and fill them with water. Now ask a friend to hold out their hands, palms down.

On the back of their hands place the 2 cups of water. Now ask them to remove the cups without spilling a drop.

The answer is very simple. Drink 1 cup of water, then remove the other with your free hand. Easy, but it can keep your friend puzzling for a long time.

...rry up... ...turn!

The tablecloth trick

How many times have you seen that famous trick where a magician pulls away the table-cloth from under all the cups, saucers and plates?

We are not suggesting that you try this trick. However, here is a simplified version which you might like to try. Even this one will take a lot of practise.

Fill a plastic mug with water, but make certain the outside of the mug is thoroughly dry otherwise it won't work.

Place the mug on a sheet of paper (a sheet of writing paper is best to start with). To make this trick work it is essential that you:

* hold the 2 corners of the paper firmly (as shown)
* pull the paper with a sharp jerk
* keep the paper straight and flat as you pull.

To perfect this trick is going to take some practice and a lot of patience. Once you have perfected it you could use an *old* glass mug to add to the effect.

Cleaning the water

During a pause in the rain, dash outside and fill a small basin with muddy water. It may be easier to bring in a handful of soil and mix it into a basin of water. Next, find a second basin about the same size as the first.

Place the basin of muddy water on a pile of books. Find a small towel (or a large handkerchief). Put one end in the muddy water and the other end in the empty basin (as shown).

Go and find something else to do for a while. When you come back you will see that the water from the top basin is trickling down the cloth into the lower basin.

Only clear water will travel into the second basin — the mud stays behind. Although the water may look clean, DON'T DRINK IT — it could contain lots of germs.